MY LITTLE PONY PIONEER

Bonnie Zacherle

MEGAN BORGERT-SPANIOL

Checkerboard
Library

An Imprint of Abdo Publishing
abdobooks.com

abdobooks.com

Published by Abdo Publishing, a division of ABDO, PO Box 398166, Minneapolis, Minnesota 55439. Copyright © 2019 by Abdo Consulting Group, Inc. International copyrights reserved in all countries. No part of this book may be reproduced in any form without written permission from the publisher. Checkerboard Library™ is a trademark and logo of Abdo Publishing.

Printed in the United States of America, North Mankato, Minnesota
102018
012019

THIS BOOK CONTAINS
RECYCLED MATERIALS

Design and Production: Mighty Media, Inc.
Editor: Katherine Hengel Frankowski
Cover Photographs: Fauquier Times (center); Mighty Media, Inc.
Interior Photographs: AP Images, p. 25; Brian Zagst at Nerfuls.org, pp. 18, 19; Cassandra Brown/FauquierNow.com, p. 17; Courtesy of The Strong, Rochester, New York, pp. 11, 28 (top); Enokson/Flickr, pp. 12, 13 (top, bottom), 28 (bottom); Everett Collection NYC, pp. 23, 26; Fauquier Times, p. 5; Getty Images, pp. 24, 27; Hina Ichigo/Flickr, pp. 21, 22, 29 (top, bottom); Mighty Media, Inc., p. 16; Shutterstock, pp. 4, 6, 7; Wikimedia Commons, pp. 8, 9; www.PonylandPress.com, p. 14–15

Library of Congress Control Number: 2018948785

Publisher's Cataloging-in-Publication Data
Names: Borgert-Spaniol, Megan, author.
Title: My Little Pony pioneer: Bonnie Zacherle / by Megan Borgert-Spaniol.
Other title: Bonnie Zacherle
Description: Minneapolis, Minnesota : Abdo Publishing, 2019 | Series: Toy
    trailblazers set 3 | Includes online resources and index.
Identifiers: ISBN 9781532117107 (lib. bdg.) | ISBN 9781532159947 (ebook)
Subjects: LCSH: Zacherle, Bonnie--Juvenile literature. | Inventors--United States--
    Biography--Juvenile literature. | My Little Pony (Trademark)--Juvenile
    literature. | Toymakers--Biography--Juvenile literature.
Classification: DDC 688.72092 [B]--dc23

CONTENTS

Chapter 1

A CHILDHOOD
Dream

Bonnie Zacherle is a creator. She is a designer and illustrator. Early in her career as an illustrator, Zacherle sketched an idea for a toy pony. She had no idea how far the idea would go.

In time, Zacherle's drawing **evolved** into the original My Little Pony toy! **Decades** later, My Little Pony is still a widely popular toy.

When Bonnie first sketched her toy pony, she was remembering her childhood. As a kid, Bonnie didn't play with many toys. What she really wanted was a horse of her own.

The Korean pony that inspired Bonnie Zacherle to create My Little Pony was named Knicker. Zacherle said her original toy ponies were chubby because Knicker was!

Bonnie was born on November 14, 1946, in Norwood, Massachusetts. Her interest in horses began at age four or five. Bonnie was living in Japan at the time. Her father was working there as a veterinarian for the US Army. His job was to look after animals coming in and out of the country.

One of the animals was a Korean pony. Bonnie fell in love with the pony. She decided she wanted a pony of her own. Years passed, and Bonnie never got a pony. Instead, she designed one that could fit in her hand. Because of Bonnie, kids everywhere can have their own little ponies!

Chapter 2

Becoming an ILLUSTRATOR

Zacherle's father influenced her love of ponies. He also influenced what Zacherle studied when she first started college. Zacherle's father wanted her to be a veterinarian, like him. So, Zacherle began college as a biology major at New York's Syracuse University.

But Zacherle did not study biology for long. Her true passion was drawing, an activity she had enjoyed since she was a child. So, Zacherle switched her major to illustration and advertising design. Zacherle's new path may not have been what her father had wanted. But she chose to do what made her happy.

In her new major, Zacherle took an interest in developing characters. She knew she wanted to be an illustrator after college. But she wasn't sure where she could put her talents to work.

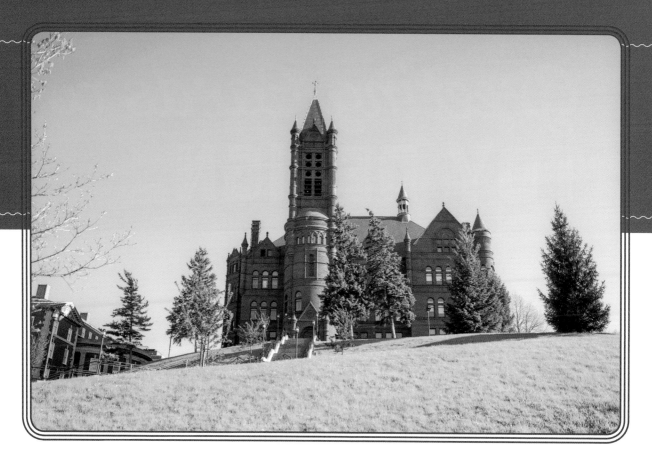

Syracuse University was the first US college where students, including Zacherle, could study fine arts.

Zacherle figured she would likely end up illustrating children's books in the future. She graduated from college in the early 1970s. She soon found a job as an illustrator. But Zacherle wasn't working on children's books. She was illustrating greeting cards!

Chapter 3

Greeting Cards to TOY DESIGN

Zacherle began working at Rust Craft Greeting Card Company in Massachusetts in 1971. As a greeting card illustrator, she practiced the art that she loved. However, she wasn't making much money. So, Zacherle decided to work as a **freelance** illustrator in addition to her regular job. This allowed her to make extra money.

As a freelance artist, Zacherle began doing illustration and design work for the toy company Hasbro in

Hasbro makes many popular toys and games. These include Jenga, Transformers, Play-Doh, and Trolls!

Rhode Island. The people at Hasbro liked Zacherle's work. They told her that if she got tired of greeting cards, she could have a job at Hasbro.

Eventually, Zacherle accepted Hasbro's offer. She left Rust Craft Greeting Card Company in 1980 to become a full-time illustrator for Hasbro. This new job marked the start of Zacherle's career in toy design. This was the type of work that would eventually make her famous!

Chapter 4
My Pretty
PONY

At Hasbro, Zacherle worked in research and development. One of her responsibilities was to come up with ideas for new toys. Zacherle began thinking about what she would have liked to play with as a kid. Her childhood dream of having a pony quickly came to mind.

Zacherle drew a line of toy horses, each small enough to fit in a child's hand. The horses looked like real pony **breeds**, such as pintos, palominos, and Appaloosas. These were the types of horses Zacherle had loved in her youth. She wanted young kids to be able to use their imaginations to pretend the toy horses were real.

In 1981, Hasbro released a larger **version** of Zacherle's design. It was called My Pretty Pony. The plastic toy was 10 inches (25 cm) tall. It was brown with white spots and had a mane and tail that kids could comb. My Pretty Pony also had mechanical parts. When a lever was pressed, the pony could wiggle its ears, swish its tail, and wink an eye!

Each My Pretty Pony came with hair care items, a red saddle blanket, and a Western hat.

Hasbro also released a second My Pretty Pony in 1981. It had a pink body and hair. It also had seven dark pink hearts on its backside. These hearts later became known as "cutie marks."

Chapter 5

PONY REDESIGN

My Pretty Pony wasn't on the **market** long before its design was changed. Hasbro **executives** felt My Pretty Pony's sales could be better. The wife of a Hasbro executive suggested the company shrink My Pretty Pony into a smaller, softer toy. Hasbro took this advice and asked Zacherle to do the redesign.

© 1983 Hasbro Ind., Inc.

Zacherle drew a new line of smaller ponies. She wanted them to look **realistic**. But Hasbro's marketing wanted to make the ponies pastel colors. Zacherle did not like this idea. But the pastel colors proved popular with a test group of kids. So, Zacherle accepted that the ponies wouldn't look exactly as she had imagined them. The redesigned pony had hair that could be combed like My Pretty Pony.

However, the updated **version** did not have mechanical parts. It was simpler than My Pretty Pony. It was also made of **vinyl**, a softer material than the hard plastic of My Pretty Pony.

In 1983, Zacherle's six updated ponies were released under the name My Little Pony. They were incredibly popular! My Little Ponies would remain popular well beyond their release. Over the next ten years, they would become one of the most successful toy lines in Hasbro's history!

Chapter 6

ORIGINAL SIX

T he first line of My Little Ponies is the first generation, or G1. Of these, the first six characters are called the "Original Six." Zacherle named each pony! They were called Blossom, Butterscotch, Blue Belle, Cotton Candy, Minty, and Snuzzle. Each had a special "cutie mark" on its backside that was designed by Zacherle.

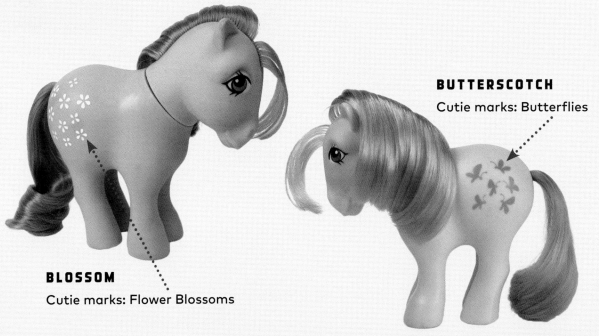

BUTTERSCOTCH
Cutie marks: Butterflies

BLOSSOM
Cutie marks: Flower Blossoms

BLUE BELLE

Cutie marks: Stars

COTTON CANDY

Cutie marks: Spots

MINTY

Cutie marks: Clover

SNUZZLE

Cutie marks: Hearts

15

Chapter 7

HASBRO TO
Parker Brothers

Zacherle's official involvement in the My Little Pony line lasted about one year. Because she designed the toy, Hasbro had to pay her for the **patent**. But Zacherle was already a paid Hasbro employee. So, this patent payment was only a **formality**. Zacherle received one dollar to sign the patent over to Hasbro. She never imagined My Little Pony would make Hasbro millions of dollars over the years!

My Little Pony wasn't the only famous toy Zacherle worked on at Hasbro. She also worked on a redesign of Mr. Potato Head. Zacherle came up with the trap door on the back of the toy for storing extra parts. She is also responsible for giving Mr. Potato Head arms!

Today, Mr. Potato Head comes with more extra parts than can fit inside it!

Zacherle in her home office with My Little Pony and Mr. Potato Head toys

Zacherle remained at Hasbro for a few years after My Little Pony came out. In 1985, she accepted a job at Parker Brothers, a toy and game company in Massachusetts. Zacherle considered this a dream job. Parker Brothers paid her more than Hasbro had. And, she got to play games all day long.

At Parker Brothers, Zacherle created a line of toys called Nerfuls. Nerfuls were characters that had balls as heads. The heads connected to plastic bodies and plastic hats or hair. Kids could **detach** the plastic parts to create different combinations.

Designing toys like Nerfuls was the kind of work Zacherle loved. But Parker Brothers was best known for the games it created. These included board games, video games, and card games. Zacherle's role at the company also included game design. And while Zacherle loved toy design, she decided that game design was not her passion. So, she left Parker Brothers in 1989.

Nerfuls slogan was "Mix 'em, match 'em, roll 'em, change 'em, pose 'em, bounce 'em. They're a ball to be around!"

In 1990, Zacherle began working for herself. She eventually teamed up with Liz Knight, a former Hasbro **colleague**.

Together, the two women did **freelance** design projects and consulting work from their own studio in Massachusetts.

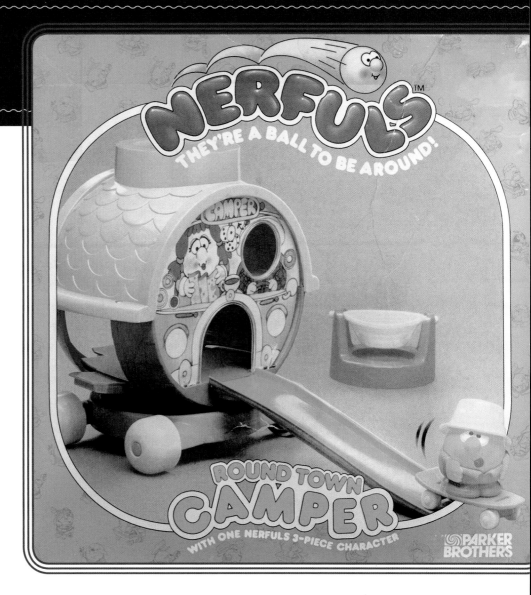

NERFULS™

THEY'RE A BALL TO BE AROUND!

CAMPER

ROUND TOWN CAMPER

WITH ONE NERFULS 3-PIECE CHARACTER

PARKER BROTHERS

Chapter 9

Pony EVOLUTION

As Zacherle's career **evolved** over the years, so did My Little Pony. After Zacherle left Hasbro, the company expanded My Little Pony beyond the Original Six. It released unicorn ponies, winged ponies, baby ponies, and more. All together, these additional ponies made up the first generation, or G1, of My Little Pony.

To promote the G1 line, Hasbro worked with an advertising agency to create TV specials featuring the ponies. The popularity of the specials led to *My Little Pony: The Movie*. The film was released by Marvel Productions in 1986. That same year, the first My Little Pony TV series aired. It was called *My Little Pony 'n Friends*.

The G1 My Little Pony line ran until 1992. In 1997, Hasbro released a new generation of My Little Ponies. The G2 ponies were smaller than the G1 line. The new generation had heads that could turn.

Several generations and variations of the My Little Pony character Applejack

Hasbro introduced the third generation of My Little Pony in 2003. The G3 line featured updated pony shapes, poses, and colors. By then, many parents who had grown up playing with the G1 ponies now had kids of their own. They could share My Little Pony with their kids through the G3 line.

Chapter 10

THE FOURTH
Generation

The most recent My Little Pony generation, G4, **debuted** in 2010. The G4 line was based on the characters from a TV series that first aired the same year. It is called *My Little Pony: Friendship Is Magic*.

Animator Lauren Faust created the TV show and G4 characters. Faust had played with the G1 toy line when she was a girl. She based her six G4 characters on her favorite G1 ponies.

My Little Pony: Friendship Is Magic renewed the popularity of the My Little Pony brand. It did so through its messages promoting kindness, honesty, generosity, and other virtues.

The TV show and G4 toy line have attracted a huge fan base.

FUN FACT

The G4 characters are named Applejack, Fluttershy, Pinkie Pie, Rainbow Dash, Rarity, and Twilight Sparkle.

Pinkie Pie

Many of these fans gather at My Little Pony **conventions**. At a 2015 convention, Zacherle and Faust met for the first time.

At the convention, fans watched Zacherle and Faust discuss My Little Pony. This was a special moment for the two women and their fans. Without Zacherle, Faust's characters and TV show wouldn't exist. And Zacherle admired what Faust had done with My Little Pony.

Chapter 11

BRONIES

When Zacherle and Faust met, they discussed how popular My Little Pony had become. People of all ages attend the various My Little Pony **conventions**. Many of them even show up in pony costumes!

One group of fans that has surprised Zacherle is adult men. When Zacherle created My Little Pony, the toy was **marketed** toward young girls. This remained the toy's target market for much of its history.

But *My Little Pony: Friendship Is Magic* changed this. The show became hugely popular among adult men who appreciate its messages about friendship. These fans call themselves Bronies. Bronies have formed a growing **online**

Brony is a combination of the words "bro" and "pony."

In 2014, more than half of all Bronies were from the United States. The average Brony age was 21.

community where they discuss the show and toys. Many Bronies show up in costume at My Little Pony **conventions** too.

Bronies have proven that adults and kids can enjoy the same toys and shows. These fans have also challenged **gender stereotypes**. Bronies are part of a larger group of people who want to change the way companies **market** toys. Today, many people are encouraging toy companies to develop toys for all kids instead of specific genders.

Chapter 12

MORE THAN
Toys

My Little Pony has come a long way since its creation. So has Zacherle. Today, she lives in Warrenton, Virginia, where she teaches art to kids. She also illustrates books, including one she wrote about creating My Little Pony. It is called *My Lil Pony Tale* and was published in 2016.

Zacherle continues to visit My Little Pony **conventions**. Each one reminds her of the many people she has inspired with her creation. She also gets to see the hundreds of different My Little Pony characters created over the past 30 years.

For Zacherle, My Little Pony's continued popularity is connected to the toy's simplicity.

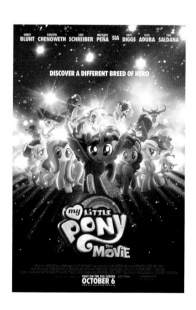

The new *My Little Pony: The Movie* came out in 2017.

My Little Pony doesn't light up, make noise, or move on its own. It is up to kids to give each pony life. This encourages kids to make up their own stories and characters. To Zacherle, this is how My Little Pony becomes more than a toy. As she says, "It becomes a friend."

TIMELINE

1946
Zacherle is born in Norwood, Massachusetts.

1981
Hasbro releases a plastic, mechanical pony called My Pretty Pony.

1985
Zacherle leaves Hasbro to design toys and games for Parker Brothers.

1980
Zacherle becomes a full-time illustrator for Hasbro.

1983
Zacherle's redesign of My Pretty Pony is released as My Little Pony. The original toy line includes six different characters.

FUN FACT

From 1986 to 1989, Hasbro sold Pony Friends. These toys resembled My Little Ponies, but were made up of elephants, giraffes, zebras, and more!

2003

Hasbro introduces the third generation of My Little Pony. It features updated pony shapes, poses, and colors.

2015

Zacherle and *Friendship Is Magic* creator Lauren Faust meet at a My Little Pony convention.

1997

The second generation of My Little Pony debuts. These ponies are smaller than the previous generation.

2010

My Little Pony: Friendship Is Magic debuts along with the fourth generation of My Little Pony.

2016

Zacherle publishes *My Lil Pony Tale*, a book about creating My Little Pony.

Glossary

animator – a person skilled in creating series of drawings that appear to move due to slight changes in each drawing.

breed – a group of animals sharing the same ancestors and appearance.

colleague – someone you work with or who does the same kind of work as you.

convention – a group of people meeting for a special purpose.

debut – to make a first appearance.

decade – a time period of ten years.

detach – to separate from a larger mass.

evolve – to develop into something else.

executive – a person with senior managerial responsibility in a business organization.

formality – an established rule.

freelance – pursuing work with an employer without being committed to work for that employer for a long time.

gender – the behaviors, characteristics, and qualities most often associated with either the male or female sex.

market – a particular type of people who might buy something. To market a product is to advertise or promote it so people will want to buy it.

online – connected to the internet.

patent – the exclusive right granted to a person to make or sell an invention. This right lasts for a certain period of time.

realistic – true to life or nature.

stereotype – an idea that many people have about a thing or a group and that may often be untrue or only partly true.

version – a different form or type of an original.

vinyl – a plastic consisting of a polymer that is commonly used to make phonograph records.